Relationship Workbook for Couples

The Ultimate Beginner's Relationship Workbook for Couples - 4-Week Action Plan Blueprint Guide to Deeper Connection, Trust, and Intimacy for Couples - Young and Old

By Isabella Evelyn

For more great books, visit:

EffingoPublishing.com

Download another book for Free

We want to thank you for purchasing this book and offer you another book (just as long and valuable as this book), "To be mentioned later," completely free.

Visit the link below to signup and receive it:

www.effingopublishing.com/gift

In this book, we will break down the most common health & fitness mistakes, you are probably committing right now, and will reveal how you can quickly get in the best shape of your life!

In addition to this valuable gift, you will also have an opportunity to get our new books for free, enter giveaways, and receive other useful emails from us. Again, visit the link to sign up:

www.effingopublishing.com/gift

TABLE OF CONTENT

Introduction 7

Chapter 1: Speak the Language of Love 10

Two-way Communication 14

Know your faults. 16

Expose feelings that are distressing or humiliating. 16

Share your wants with your partner. 17

It's not about you every time. 19

Listen to your partner 19

Show that you are listening 20

Empathize with your partner. 20

Useful Communicating Advice 22

Intimidation: A General Relationship Problem 22

Parental Communication 23

Communicating Non-Verbally in a Relationship 24

Chapter 02: What fruit does the Relationship produce? 26

The difference between Falling in Love & Staying in Love 34

It all starts with you. 37

Attention 37

Take it Easy 38

Chapter 03: Rekindle the Intimacy in a Relationship 40

Ways to Restore Intimacy in a Relationship 47

Chapter 04: Re-sparkling the Flame of Ownership 56

What is Ownership in a Relationship? 58

Why is it important? 58

It avoids Unhealthy Conflicts 59

How lack of ownership spoils a healthy relationship? 60

Ways to Practice Ownership in Real Life 62

Chapter 05: Attitudes of Gratitude & Appreciation in a Relationship 69

Gifts like chocolate and flowers (for men!) 79

Focus on minute details 80

Disrupt the conventional routine 80

Show gratitude on your success 81

Be Consistent 82

Conclusion 83

Final Words 84

About the Co-Authors 86

Introduction

What are the fundamentals of a healthy and successful relationship? Commitment, passion, and appreciation are all essential—yet without specific elementary skills, even the most committed and loyal companion can find themselves declining into quarrels, arguments, and disappointment. With the help of this "Relationship workbook for Couple," Effingo Publishing presents a useful guide for building a successful partnership based on trust and cooperation—proposing relationship saving procedures and on-spot conflict resolution strategies for avoiding the heated arguments that most commonly break relationships apart

In this friendly and easy to use workbook the Effingo Publishing teaches you

Speak the language of Love—understanding why communication is essential among the couples

What fruit does the Relationship produce—Analyzing why understanding your partner is the topmost quality of a right partner in a dreamy relationship

***Rekindle the Intimacy in a Relationship*—** learning about common intimacy issues can help lovers to work through their complications

***Re-sparkling the Flame of Ownership*--** It allows your partner to exercise the right of their free will.

***Attitudes of Gratitude & Appreciation in a Relationship*—**Understanding how gratitude and appreciation will help you to rejuvenate the relationship.

The 'Relationship workbook for Couple' has transformed numerous relationships. Its ideas are basic and conveyed with clarity, making this book as practical as possible. You will be intrigued by its straightforward approach. Reading this book will feel like conversing with best friends. Applying it will protect your relationship—starting today

Also, before you get started, I recommend you joining our email newsletter to receive updates on any upcoming new book releases or promotions. You can sign-up for free, and as a bonus, you will receive a gift. I wish you all the best for buying this book "Relationship Workbook for Couple," I am sure this book will help you manage your relationships.

The book consists of chapters that will provide you with the visions that can be very beneficial to you in successfully managing your relationships. It will give you the number of tools and strategies to make you accomplish your relationship goals. It will allow you to learn more about yourself; the type of person you are also will help in understanding personalities different from you.

The book was specifically designed to clear many concepts of relationship. It is a straightforward yet beneficial book for all those who are struggling in a relationship. It consists of a couple of exercises that will help you sort out your relationship problems. It will cover all the aspects that make the relationship unsuccessful. The exercises in this book will help you clarify your relationship goals.

There are a plethora of books available in the market with the same subject. Thank you so much for allowing us to help you with your problems. We intend to provide as much useful information as possible. Enjoy reading the book.

Once again, to join our free email newsletter and to receive a free copy of this valuable book, please visit the link and signup now: www.effingopublishing.com/gift.

Chapter 1: Speak the Language of Love

Many people never get a chance to learn how to communicate. Without having this skill, the individual finds it impossible to survive in an intimate relationship. Without expressing themselves and listening to another, partners cannot reach intimacy. By enhancing your communication skills, the individual and the partner will be able to institute and maintain a loving, healthy relationship between two individuals who love each other.

Why is communication important in a Relationship?

One of the most common problems in communicating with each other is that couples misconstrued why communication is essential. Many people conceive it as a debate in which every individual represents a preconceived description of the reality about what is happening between the two partners.

The mistake with this approach is the preconceived assumption that either individual can go into the discussion with an accurate opinion of reality. It is not possible because not everyone has the compulsory facts to determine what reality is, that is: what is going on between the partners.

One of the reasons why communication is important is to determine reality. Communication includes the collaboration of two individuals as they share and analyze all of their perceptions, emotional states, ideas, and opinions to come to an accurate understanding of what is happening.

The most common communication mistakes that can break down the association in your relationship are.

1. Screaming & Yelling

If you are in a relationship for quite some time, you are most likely going to end up raising your voice against them. But if that has become a habit between the two of you, you might be producing more problems than you can solve.

2. Being Sorry all the time.

Saying sorry after every disagreement or conflict might seem like a safe bet, but it can essentially become quite a concern in your relationship. People apologize simply to get their lover off their backs, or to stop being yelled at. However, this eventually communicates to your lover that they can act unbearably to you, and you will be the one who apologizes.

3. The Reticence

While it may seem understandable that an adult relationship shouldn't involve the same communication skills you used on the playground in second grade, relationship experts want you to know how risky the silent treatment is.

4. Self-Assumptions

It's natural to expect certain behavior from your partner, but making assumptions and then sharing them can become damaging. Assumptions are detrimental to any relationship. In a relationship, it's imperative to understand that your rules or expectations in a relationship aren't universal and need to be communicated to your lover. It can help both get what they want or need from the association and can create an incredibly pleasing, gratifying relationship

5. Not asking

When you are in a relationship with someone, that doesn't mean they can read your mind. It means that not asking for what you need can become the main barrier to a healthy relationship. "When it comes to what you want out of an association, there are many explanations you may not want to be completely honest and even hypocritical sometimes.

Although this can become the source of a lot of misapprehensions. This sort of bumpy situation can occur at all stages of a relationship if you aren't open about your wants. There's no way to be on the same page as your partner if you aren't honest.

6. *Not discussing the Issue*

If you have a pet peeve or anything in the relationship is bothering you, you must bring it up sooner rather than later.

Next time you have an issue with your partner skipping out on date night, or when he/she won't text you back for hours at a time, bring it in front of them after you've had time to dig deep inside and find out the reason why it's bugging you.

Perhaps, you were hurt in a former relationship. Perhaps, you feel like you're being put second. Bringing up larger themes will help your lovers understand and connect with you on a deeper level. Plus, it'll help you avoid bigger problems like screaming matches and silent treatments down the line.

7. Lack of Interest

If you can't find a way to communicate backing for your lover and their ideas, your relationship can fail and become unsuccessful

Two-way Communication

Everybody has a fair idea that communication involves talking and listening to each other. Although many of us inaccurately believe that communication is very easy and simple. When we start thinking like this, we don't realize that rather than including inborn abilities, communication also includes particular skills that can be acquired and established in ourselves to communicate with and actively listen to people we love. Some of the basic steps are mentioned below:

- *Step 1: Starting a conversation with your loved one.*
- *Step 2: Speaking to your loved one*
- *Step 3: Actively Listening to your loved one*
- *Step 4: Defining reality with your loved one*

Step 1: Starting a Conversation with Your loved one

The basic rule to follow when in a conversation with your loved ones: Don't prove yourself. That is, forget about being right all the time!! It's a conversation, not a battle that you have to win.

Here, I don't mean to compromise on everything. All I am saying is that you can't be annoyed, angry, or triggered. You can be correct in all of your opinions and feelings. But the point is learning to disagree.

Just imagine that the person you love might have something to say that is worth paying attention to, and considering. The conversation between two people should be a conversation; the discussion should not reach up to the point of fighting with each other.

Step 2: Speaking to your loved one

If you are having a conversation with the person you love, remember that there is only one reality that an individual can be sure of: you are only familiar with your feelings, thoughts, and perceptions. You have no idea about the other person's thoughts, feelings, or perceptions. Try to understand this thing.

The only thing that is much needed is to talk about something common. When you are talking about something common, the chances are that everyone is familiar with the reality of what is going on between two individuals. I am not saying don't talk about anything that isn't common. First, start the conversation with common points and try to gain confidence before starting to talk about something uncommon.

Know your faults.

It is an ill-fated reality that, within almost every other couple, only one person becomes the victim by the other. As a result, the emphasis of many of their conversations or discussions is to blame each other. In a conversation, always avoid the temptation to diverge into criticizing, attacking, accusing, or blaming your partner.

Expose feelings that are distressing or humiliating.

It is indeed essential to identify your illogical feelings. Don't let them go considering them incorrect, meaningless, or immature. Try to talk about the illogical feeling that you rather skip. The feelings that you think are embarrassing or humiliating should you disclose them.

For example, if you feel offended or upset, talk over these feelings with your partner. Don't think of defending yourself by becoming the victim and virtuous. It is not about how you shouldn't be offended or upset. It is just about letting the other person know that you are hurt, and it causes emotional pain.

Share your wants with your partner.

Many people find it hard to talk about what they want. I am not talking about simple wants like I want to try the new restaurant. I want to buy a leather jacket etc. etc. The personal wants I am talking about are the deep down wants in you where you become the most vulnerable like I want you to appreciate me, I want to be friendly with you, I want to start a family with you.

Many people feel ashamed or embarrassed about their wants. Although these are the things that should bring into a discussion with your loved ones, the more that you communicate, the more your partner will feel the sense of importance.

When you and your loved one connect on this level, many of the insignificant issues between you evaporate. It becomes apparent that they were merely inconsequential issues meant to distract you in your relationship.

In the last, talk to your loved one with the courtesy and respect with which you speak to anyone else.

Many people have a particular way of communicating that they spare for their partners. What makes it special is that it consists of offensive behaviors like being whining, complaining, irritating, behaving childish, and many other behaviors like these.

When you are in a conversation with your partner, stop and question yourself: "Would I be talking like this to anyone else?" "Do you hear yourself complaining or demanding in any way" or deferring?

Always treat your loved ones with respect. Treat them in a way; you want to be treated

Step 3: Actively Listening to your loved one

When in a conversation, you have very little mindfulness of what your loved one thinks and feels. You might think you do because you identify an expression that he-she always catches when he-she is hurt. Or you may have even switched over some heated words. But if you haven't listened to your partner, you know nothing.

Listening actively or attentively is a skill that needs to be acquired and established. Just because we heard something does not mean that we have listened to it. Active listening involves an unconditional interest in understanding the person who is talking to us. By doing this, we truly get to know that person.

It's not about you every time.

Listening is completely about the person you are paying attention to. Don't mix your point of view. Your opinions, thoughts, or reactions to what the other individual is telling are both irrelevant and incorrect. The person is telling you all this is not seeking your advice or guidance. What they need is to be heard so that they feel that they are being understood.

Listen to your partner

When you don't mix your thoughts, feelings, or opinions, you start to focus on what your partner is saying instead of how you are reacting, and make yourself available to listen to your partner. Try to understand their problem by stepping in their shoe.

Try to feel what the other person is experiencing. Feel it. Make an effort to empathize with what your loved one is presently feeling while talking with you.

Show that you are listening

It is not enough to listen quietly. It is useful to show to your loved one that you are hearing. While in a conversation, replicate what your partner is mentioning and feeling. Repeat to them what you hear and tell them that you are actually listening and understanding them, and not just sitting quietly.

If your replication is not proper, your lover can correct you. You can then make alterations until you have a correct understanding of what your partner is trying to tell you. Reflecting or replicating or asking questions, lets your partner know that he or she is being heard, which gives them a sense of satisfaction.

Empathize with your partner.

As you listen to your loved one with empathy and feel what the other one is feeling, you acquire compassion for the other person. You feel for your partner as a human being with individual pain and scuffles like the rest of us.

You develop a different perspective. When you understand or feel your partner's issues, your issues seem insignificant. Giving advice to your partner or being disapproving quickly seems arrogant and pompous. Behaving hurt or victimized quickly seems childish and self-indulgent. From this new perspective, you see your loved one as a separate person who you care the most as the person deals with his-her own issues in life.

Step 4: Defining reality with your loved one

In the process of speaking about your self as your loved one has actually listened, it is like that both the individuals come across a fair understanding of what you have experienced and felt. Likewise, as your loved one spoke personally to you, having you listening allows you to come across a deep understanding of the experiences and feelings of your loved one.

This level of perception and understanding, along with the ability to empathize and compassion that comes with it, help simplify much of the confusion that exists between a couple. The deeper mindfulness of each other eradicates many of the misinterpretations of misconceptions and miscommunications that creates confusion. What stays is a clearer picture of yourselves and the genuineness of your relationship.

When you reach this point of conversation, you and your loved one might want to analyze what you have cultured about yourselves and each other and your relationship. By discussing what you have learned, you can recognize the personal concerns and reactions that lead to trouble between you. You will now understand what to look out for to avoid any problem in future. And if you do get into trouble, you can identify what is happening, and you can easily deal with it more rapidly.

Useful Communicating Advice

There are many negative practices of communication to be aware of. Make sure not to indulge in any of these because they infect the communication process. As long as you are considering these techniques and procedures, you can be sure that you and your lover will become more and more separate and on bad terms with each other.

Communication should allow you and your lover to come close to each other. Communication should break down the obstacles that keep you apart, not to build up barricades between you.

Intimidation: A General Relationship Problem

One of the most effective practices that couples use to influence, govern, and punish each other is intimidation. As per the dictionary, the meaning of intimidating is to scare into submission.

Surprisingly enough, couples report that intimidating behaviors are not those that are obvious and hostile. Instead, partners are scared by the indirect, covert behaviors that leave them feeling embarrassed and responsible for their partner's unhappiness.

In a conversation between a couple, if one person responds by being unhappy, self-hating, or self-destructive, it is almost impossible for the other person not to submit. The conversation is over; the person intimidating has won the discussion.

But the reality is different, both the persons have suffered tragic defeats. As per the dictionary, to intimidate "infers reduction to a state where the soul is broken or all courage vanishes." This certainly means the emotional state of the person who has been scared into submission. Similarly, the cost to intimidating partner is also high. The intimidating person must lose his or her autonomy, after which the soul is broken, and courage vanishes.

Parental Communication

Look for ways that you may be communicating from a childish stance. Such communications include submitting and surrendering, watching for direction or definition, being submissive or obedient, seeking support and/or criticism.

Parental interactions include directing and controlling, being superior and assertive, acting judgmental and serious.

None of these abilities has a place in the communications between two Lovers/ adults in an equal relationship. Be very respectful of yourself and highly respectful of your lover, in the way you communicate with each other.

Communicating Non-Verbally in a Relationship

Non-verbal communication means how a person's body language participates in the process of communicating a state of mind and reactions. Non-verbal communication is not a destructive form of communication. On the contrary, it can be beneficial in trying to understand what your loved one is saying.

Many times what the other person is saying does not match with what he or she is communicating as non-verbally. The mix of these messages sometimes creates confusion. All you need to do is to acknowledge both the messages, even if they don't resemble. After this, decide which message communicates the exact meaning of what the other person is trying to convey. Nonverbal messages sometimes have more meanings and more accurate.

Most of these messages are communicated in some relationships. A partner saying, "I love you" throughout the day and behave uninterestedly and unresponsively. A partner may show interest and concerns about a lover, but every time the mate speaks about him-herself, the partner intrudes or becomes unfocused.

Always pay attention to what your actions are portraying. Make sure to match your words and actions. In simple words, be genuine in how you communicate both verbally and non-verbally.

Chapter 02: What fruit does the Relationship produce?

There is a specific reason why Understanding your partner is one of the topmost qualities of a good lover in a dreamy relationship. Apart from the fact that understanding allows your loved one to be who they want to be without being judged all the time, it offers you see things from a different perspective

If you're having any problem to know how to become a more understanding lover in a relationship, this chapter will help you identify, appreciate, and practice such an important characteristic of a good lover.

Some ways to become more understanding in a relationship are:

1. Find some time to know each other

The trial of trying to understand the other person lies in a person's inability to see them not just as a lover but also as a human being who is capable of dissimilar feelings and emotions. It's quite impossible to learn how to understand your loved one if you don't know them: By knowing them, I meant their strengths, their pleasures, their doubts, and also their imperfections.

As a lover, you have to take some time out to get to know your partner better. It may take months or years, but it's worth knowing your partner, especially if you want your relationship to stay longer

2. Be cautious of your moods and feelings.

Learning how to understand the other person can be challenging if you don't even recognize yourself. How well do you understand yourself? What are the things that make you pleased, unhappy, or angry? How do these feelings provoke you? How do they help you in making decisions? If you know the answers to all these questions about yourself, then it can be easier for you to identify your partner and recognize their struggle.

If you have the potential to understand yourself, then you can easily understand the other person.

3. Never force your standards and beliefs.

It doesn't matter if you think you are better than your lover as far the experience, maturity, or even in intellect is concerned, never force your standards and beliefs. By doing so, you will become a blind person who cannot see past his nose.

If you want to be an understanding lover in a relationship, you should identify that respecting your partner's own beliefs and accepting their convictions as a part of who they are, are essential if you want to keep your relationship healthier.

4. Allow your lover to live a life outside of the relationship. (Give some space)

Being an understanding lover means identifying that your relationship is not the only thing your partner has – and it goes the same with your loved one. In simpler words, never force your lover to make their relationship number one priority – and it includes giving them space, the freedom just to live and have fun, even if you're not with them.

5. Respect your Lover's needs as a social being.

Let your lover go out with their friends or let them spend time with their family as well. Allow them to travel alone and permit them to live their life to the fullest, even if you are not around. Most significantly, they allow them to pursue their personal goals and motivate them to go out into the world and achieve their dreams.

6. You cannot be right all the time.

In contrast to the previous part, being an understanding lover means actively listening to what the other person has to say. You can't always be right; stop trying to prove that your opinions, ideas, and judgment are more acceptable. As it can hurt your lover more and can even lead to an argument.

7. Learn to Cooperate

If you want to be an understanding partner, you must find common ground. Instead of blaming each other, try to analyze that your partner is not your enemy. Look for something that you both can agree upon. Not only will it avoid your conflicts, but it also will increase the love between you.

8. Give Some time to clarify before responding.

When you think that your lover did something that made you feel annoyed, upset, or dissatisfied, give them a chance to clarify. Hear their side of the story or their opinion, and don't be so quick on judging your partner. Sometimes, couples in a relationship tend to become angry and react damaging expressive outbursts before actually understanding their partner.

9. Try to understand the intentions or motivations.

Trying to understand, especially when your companion did something wrong, perhaps is the most perplexing thing to do, especially in cases when you feel hurt and betrayed. However, you have to find the courage and the love to understand the intentions behind, with full honesty. Most significantly, you have to have faith in your loved one and give him/her a chance to understand their intentions and motivations behind their actions.

10. Don't choose anger over kindness.

In contrast to the previous sections, in case if you find your partner to be at fault, you always have to be very kind and think about resolving the matter, rather than making it worse. Anger will never resolve any problem, especially if your loved one has done something that could end your relationship.

Anger is a normal response to an event or an action that hurts you, but it's the wrong path, specifically if you want to repair a dying relationship. To be more understanding means to be kind and gentle, it will not only heal you but will also save your doomed relationship

11. Help them to learn from mistakes and move on.

Being empathetic is one of the ways to repair an almost broken relationship. It will help you settle and understand that everybody can make mistakes, so is your partner. Believe that they deserve the second chance to prove themselves once again.

By doing this, you have done your part in the relationship by helping your loved one learn from their mistakes. Be very patient and understanding and give it another chance. Most significantly, try to focus on their effort rather than the mistakes that they made.

12. Encourage each other to be more open.

Not many of us know how to put their thoughts and feelings into words, and this reality sometimes becomes a disputed matter, especially in a romantic relationship. First of all, how can you appreciate someone if they don't even know how to express their opinions and share their deepest feelings? In this situation, try to be more patient.

13. Keep Intimacy Alive

Touch is a basic part of human existence. Studies on infants have proved the importance of regular, loving contact for brain development. And the benefits are countless and are not limited to only childhood. Affectionate physical contact augments the body's levels of oxytocin, a hormone that impacts bonding and attachment.

However, sex is generally a foundation of a committed relationship; it shouldn't be the only way of physical intimacy. Frequent, affectionate physical contact like holding hands, hugging, kissing—is essentially important.

Of course, it's imperative to be sensitive to what your lover likes. Unwanted physical contact or inappropriate approaches can make the other individual tense up and retreat—precisely what you don't want. As with so many other aspects of a successful relationship, this can come down to how well you converse your needs and intentions with your lover.

Even if you have persistent workloads or young kids to worry about, you can help to keep physical intimacy alive by sparing some regular couple time, whether that's in the form of a dinner date or simply an hour at the end of the day where you can sit and talk or hold hands of your partner.

14. Be prepared for Ups & Downs

It's imperative to identify that there are ups and downs in every relationship. You won't always be on the same side. Sometimes one person in a relationship may be struggling with a problem that stresses them, like the death of a relative. Other occasions, like job-related problems or severe health problems, can affect both the persons in a relationship and make it problematic to relate to each other. You may have different ideas about managing your finances or raising kids. Many people cope with stress differently, and misapprehensions can rapidly turn to anger and frustration.

Don't take out your hitches on your partner. Life worries can make us short-tempered. If you are handling a lot of pressure, it may seem easier to vent with your partner, and even feel harmless to snap at them. Fighting like this might feel like a good release, but it is a slow poison to your relationship. Discover other healthier ways to manage your anger, stress, and frustration.

Trying to impose a solution can cause even bigger problems. Every person works through glitches and issues in their way. Consider yourself as a team. Persistent to move forward together can get you through the bumpy spots.

The difference between Falling in Love & Staying in Love

For many people, falling in love typically seems just to happen. It's staying in love—or maintaining that "falling in love" experience—that requires effort and commitment. Considering its rewards, though, it's worth putting the efforts. A healthy, safe romantic relationship can serve as an ongoing source of support and contentment in your life, in good times and bad, strengthening all factors of your wellbeing. By taking necessary steps now to maintain or rekindle your falling in love experience, you can build a healthy relationship that lasts—even for a whole lifetime.

Generally, couples emphasize their relationship only when there are certain, unavoidable issues to overcome. Once the complications have been resolved, they often revert their attention to their kids, careers, or other interests. Although romantic relationships demand ongoing attention and commitment for love to progress. As long as the success of a romantic relationship remains important to you, it is going to need your attention and effort. And recognizing and fixing a small issue in your relationship now can often help prevent it from expanding into a much larger one down the road.

Encourage your loved one to be more open, specifically about the things that can directly or indirectly affect your relationship. By doing so, you'll have the exact and transparent level of understanding about how you can deal with whatever unexpected situations that you'll face every day as a couple.

You keep on listening that women and men don't operate at the same time. Men are more inclined towards logic, and women are more driven by their emotions. Is it something to discuss? Are we different from each other? The answer is an emphatic YES! These variances do exist in many cases and have aided in the ongoing communication gap that infects our relationships.

Some of you might be thinking, "well, if we know we are different, should we not be able to use that to our advantage in creating more harmony and better communication?" I wish if it was that simple! But hang on, it is that easy. We have over made this issue more complicated for far too long. We continue to have unhappy males and females dragging along in their relations simply because neither truly appreciates the other. So how do we begin to put an end to this problem?

How do you take the mandatory steps to solve this issue finally? Consider the following tips when trying to get on the same page as your loved one.

It all starts with you.

Don't think I am wrong; I completely understand that your loved one has done plenty to make you upset and contribute to making a situation worse. I understand that you have made many efforts to rectify things, yet they seem to resist them, and nothing so far has worked. Despite all such situations, we as human beings will never be able to understand each other if all we do is point the finger at your loved ones. Being focused on defending your actions and pointing out their shortcomings will work against you. You are so occupied with yourself that you will then make it much harder to understand their reasoning, their needs, or their issues.

With that being said, the first step is to emphasize only what you can control, and that is you. Yes, you might have done plenty already, but can you decently say you have continued to be the person your loved one need you to be? Hold yourself responsible for your actions, and believe that by putting your best foot forward, you will give yourself a much better chance to appreciate your loved one and giving them the example they need to be a better lover as well.

Attention

Communication is the main key, although many tend to neglect the significance of non-verbal communication. Men and women already speak various languages. Therefore, a couple can communicate all day and still not be on the same page. That's why it is essential to be mindful of body language. Many times, what our loved one likes or dislikes becomes more evident when we take into account their activities and reactions in specific situations.

So, it's better to open your ears and eyes to get more in tune with your lover. Also, understand that both people in a relationship have things that they will just have a hard time fully explaining. Some girls might not tell their partners everything because she figures they should know it out on their own. Many men will also hold things back because they don't want to deal with the specific backlash they think they might receive. That's why actions are more important than words, and we need to become more attentive to both verbal and non-verbal communication.

Take it Easy

We live in a world where we like things quick and convenient. If we have to wait for something, we abandon what it is we are searching for, and we move on to the next. Well, understanding your lovers might not work that way. You are involved with an individual who has been through years of programming, that's called their life. To break all that down and truthfully understand who they are is not a race, but a marathon. People have to understand that these things take time, and it takes even longer the more an individual might do something to damage the current situation and create a more significant gap between the two individuals (Don't try to become a part of that negative cycle)

The problem is that many people don't even understand themselves, which is why getting to appreciate and understand them can become yet a more significant challenge. Take it easy and focus more on embracing progress. Learning how to understand, value, and encourage the progress will breed more growth, and before you even know it, you will be at the finishing line a lot quicker than most of the people.

There is still much more to discuss when it comes to an understanding of your partner; I would suggest, embrace these main principles that will guide you in the right direction. The goal should not be to understand every man and woman, but it should be understanding the partner you are living with. That should be the focus. By doing so, you will see a significant difference in your relationship that is full of positivity, love, enjoyment, and satisfaction.

Chapter 03: Rekindle the Intimacy in a Relationship

Intimacy in a relationship involves physical and emotional interaction. It differs from person to person. For some of us, intimacy is very easy. But for many people, it triggers opinions and actions that make intimacy painful. Many intimacy problems cause relationships to end. Many intimacy problems are not ingrained in phobias or related to Intimacy disorders.

Some intimacy problems arise when a couple becomes sexually active. Some problems come when a couple becomes emotionally intimate. Some of them begin to face intimacy issues as they mature, which can be due to other health problems or demonstrative and psychological issues.

Irrespective of the severity of the problem, there is help to cater to this. Many times, learning about common intimacy issues can help lovers to work through their complications. For example, you might find that a medical exam discloses health problems that are wreaking mess on your sex life. Or, you might be in a spell of depression or anxiety that negatively influences your relationship. Finding a qualified therapist or reading a guidebook can help put intimacy problems into perspective and help you and your lover find the answers and make changes to save the dying relationship.

Some of the secret signs that depict you have intimacy issues are:

1) You are always Angry

There are many categories of anger, and it helps to solve what type you are expressing. A deep, unconscious fear of intimacy can rear its ugly head, to show up in response to a relationship that is becoming awkwardly close, and one way this fear can become noticeable is via anger. The continuous explosions of anger is a sign of immaturity, and it becomes really hard for immature people to involve in an intimate relationship

We all lose our temper on various occasions, but if you find feelings of anger bubbling up continuously, or inappropriately, a fear of intimacy may be lurking inside the mind. The fix may not be real quick, or easy, but speaking your feelings out to your partner can help. You better share these feelings with your partner instead of allowing them to implode inside you.

2) Nobody is Perfect, Stop being one

We all want to be loved and want to feel special, but nobody is willing to trust their partner. "People in relationships are continuously asking themselves, in one way or another, if they can trust their partner. Are they allowed to show their flaws, or risk being embarrassed? The way to move past this distress is to take calculated risks. Being loved for who you are is something out of the world, but you have to show your partner your real self. Give your lover the chance to show up for you, and see how it works out. If it goes perfectly as planned, the risk for something bigger and more important. It's a perfect way to help the other person relax and be more open. Consider the example, if you say 'I doubt you won't respect, love, or find me attractive if I share this,' It lets your partner express an inclination not to reject you," Understand that nobody's perfect. No matter how good you are, or might have done something in the past, becoming clean about it will free you from the fear. Allow emotional intimacy to take the place of fear. Just replace all your fears with emotional intimacy.

3) *Being sexually Immature*

Maybe you like having sex, but you can't bond with your partner during it—ever. If that's the case, your intimacy problems may be raised to a level of sexual immaturity, which has nothing to do with your actual age. "Sexual immaturity can arise as an extreme interest in porn, or in sexual activities, as opposed to making love. Sexually immature people may also force upon using toys, or the accessories of sex, rather than focusing on their partner. It involves inattention to the partner's needs, and the whole concentration on their own need for sexual release, or satisfaction

All such people having a fear of intimacy might also hesitate from sex altogether. Both sides of the spectrum depict an inability to set free emotionally or to communicate warmly. Allow yourself to be emotionally naked towards each other; it shows that you are not afraid to bring up your fears and insecurities. Think that you can be like this all your life in almost every aspect of it, then why not sexually. Always remember that by doing this, you are allowing your partner to see your real colors & it's the best path that leads to intimacy and love.

4) *You are not connecting your soul.*

You can share a house and still have intimacy problems. Perhaps, it's the Netflix that is always on, even when you are having dinner, or the games you constantly play on your own, in the gaming room. Try to connect with a soul. It's completely normal to spare some time for yourself but understand your limits. Watching TV all day, and playing games, without involving your partner in it can make the situation worse. Physical contacts, including cuddling, staying off from the television, or a warm hug, can create a connection of the soul. Use such expressions of intimacy to communicate with your partner; it results in safety and deeper intimacy.

5) *You are a workaholic*

Being a workaholic is not a sign of honor, but rather, maybe a strong sign of emotional intimacy issues. Worse, long working hours can be tough on your physical health as well. When we burden ourselves in busywork, it may be because we are unintentionally avoiding intimacy. Many people who want to avoid intimacy burden themselves with work because they are trying to escape feelings of unhappiness, embarrassment, or anger. By staying busy all day, you can easily avoid those feelings, and ignore having to deal with them. If you are in a relationship, it's quite easy to have a routine and dodge intimate moments. By doing so will force your partner to understand that you are avoiding him/her. So, there is nothing to gain from being a workaholic all the time. Instead of being one, you should spend some time with your partner and involve in a sexual relationship; it will not only allow you to save your relationship, but having good sex will also be very good for your mental health.

6) *You keep your loved ones away from your friends & family.*

Keeping your loved ones away from your friends & family is a clear indication of a fear of intimacy. It allows you to stay segmented in a way, almost certain to eliminate true, full knowledge of who you are. Your behavior may be powered by the anxiety of shame about your old self. Perhaps, you were heavier (or clumsier, or not so good looking in school) than you want to let on, or perhaps you don't want to share your family's confined secrets with someone who is new in the family. No matter what the reason is, it's questionable that you can go the distance in a romantic relationship, and never allow them to know about your family or your past.

7) *You are not familiar*

The intimate relationship is all about knowing your partner. It involves knowing each other up to the deepest level. If you are having any intimacy issues in a relationship, it means you are not familiar with your partner. All you need to do is to identify something your partner likes or value. If you begin to understand your partner, it will certainly remove the inevitable differences amongst you.

8) *Safety of a relationship*

Many times the intimacy problems occur when there is no safety in a relationship. Both the individuals in a relationship just need to accept their differences. To have intimacy, it's not mandatory that two individuals must have the same personality. Understand each other's opinion as they look at it as an opportunity to rekindle the intimacy.

9) *You are not accepting*

Humans are designed in such a way that they don't easily accept the change. It's quite a common intimacy issue; the people in a relationship don't accept each other. We need to understand the fact that everybody is different from the other. It takes time for someone to change themselves. The minor differences can be accommodated when a person unconditionally accepts his/her partner.

10) You are not a Problem-Solver

Many people in a relationship don't have the capability to resolve their issues. As a result, it becomes one of the prominent intimacy issues. Everybody has some sort of problem in a relationship, but that should not become the reason for separation. We must learn to solve the problem before it takes a wrong turn. The individuals in a relationship must be on the same page, instead of competing with each other.

The solution is quite simple. Try to change yourself about what you wish to hide, biting the bullet, and arrange a get together with a friend or relative. Start with one individual, instead of waiting for Thanksgiving dinner. Don't worry, you'll be more likely to work yourself up to full family gatherings, and full intimacy, after some time. Make sure you're not embarrassed by any of these situations. Don't listen to all such people who wish to spoil your relationship.

Ways to Restore Intimacy in a Relationship

As the famous saying says, "it takes two to tango," it is quite certain that relationship requires both the individuals to be honest, mature, faithful, and non-judgmental. Some of the ways to restore intimacy in a relationship are mentioned as follows.

As the saying goes, it takes two to tango. Solving intimacy issues very generally requires both people to be honest, open, considerate, and non-judgmental. It also may involve one or both people to allow themselves to feel 'vulnerable.' Here are some ways to get things started.

1) Improve your communication skills

Speaking about issues is sometimes one of the best things you can do. By sharing your concerns and worries, a couple may be able to resolve their problems related to intimacy. Be aware that effective communication is always a two-way street — it's more about listening other rather than speaking

2) Working on the problem

It's quite easier to connect or feel closer to someone with whom you haven't had an argument or heated conversation. The ability to manage the feelings of hate or anger with a cool attitude is the main key to restoring intimacy.

3) Involve in combined activities

Just keep this popular saying in mind, the lovers who play together stay together. Look for something that you both enjoy doing. It could be anything from watching TV to playing chess, anything that you both feel comfortable in. Just increase the frequency of involvement in all such activities. It can be the simple most thing, and it doesn't necessarily have to be a dinner in an expensive restaurant; just a casual walk, full of love, can resolve most of your problems.

4) Talk to a close friend

Sometimes, the best advice from a friend can help to save the dying relationship. Nowadays, couples generally have a lot of mutual friends. Such friends are familiar with both the individuals in a relationship. A piece of useful advice from them can save the relationship, and a person or both the individuals in a relationship also don't get offended when a friend is explaining the ways to save their relationship.

5) Choose sensibly

The basic rule for having an intimate relationship is to choose sensibly in the first place. If being in the relationship with your boyfriend or girlfriend demands you are giving up who you really are, that you always accommodate, or that you make essential changes to be acceptable, then the person is not for you. Also, if your partner continuously accuses, blames, or bothers you or demands you are not staying close to other friends. You must Cut your losses. Get out. Make yourself accessible for someone who will honor and cherish you and appreciate you for who you are.

6) Show your true colors

As a new relationship cultivates, gradually show your true colors to each other – both the most attractive colors and the not so attractive features about you. Be open to expose your core beliefs, ethics, and ideas to find out the other's reactions. However, opposites attract each other. Still, Opposites might attract initially, but often they become the seeds of dissatisfaction as a relationship grows over time. Discover your differences and decide if they are interested or excited about you. Make sure that your dissimilarities don't violate core beliefs for either person.

7) Mark a circle

Intimacy implicates that your relationship with your partner is somehow different from your relationships with others. Many people mark the boundary around their sexual exclusivity. While others explain their intimacy in different ways. Whatever definition about fidelity you have, there needs to be something you both approve, and that is the core of what makes your bond special, valuable, and unique from all others. Both individuals must agree that making a boundary is so essential that violating it would shake the basic foundation of your relationship.

8) Cultivate emotional mindfulness

Emotions shouldn't be classified as good or bad. But how we direct them can either augment or damage intimacy. Predictably, many of you will feel angry, offended, or frustrated at times, perhaps even more. Intimacy demands to learn ways to express such feelings that are neither threatening nor distancing. Work together to explore ways to calm your intense feelings rather than getting caught up in them. Decide to work on identifying and addressing the root cause of problems instead of igniting or withdrawing.

9) Embrace the conflict

Yes, embrace it. avoiding conflict rarely works as a means to improve intimacy. Whatever the conflict was about, it just goes undiscussed, festers, and ultimately comes out in unattractive and often aggressive ways. Conflict is a sign that there is a problem that needs to be resolved. Intimacy entails facing problems with audacity and with the faith that the relationship is more essential than whatever problem is going on at the moment.

10) Be the one; you look for

It's easy to expect someone else to be understanding, empathetic, faithful, kind, and generous. But, It's not an easy job to become. Intimacy entails that we must do our very best to be the person worth being intimate with. Although, It's not necessary to be perfect at all. It is obligatory to do our best and to be very open to criticism when we miss the mark.

11. Change the pattern of initiating sex

Perhaps, you are rebuffing your lover or coming on too harsh. Avoid such criticism towards each other and don't get yourself in the "blame game." Merge things up to end the power scuffle. For example, people who are sexually active may want to practice initiating sex more frequently, and pursuers try to discover ways to tell their lover "you're sexy" in refined ways, avoiding criticism and demands for closeness at the same time.

12. Believe in affectionate touch

Offer to give your lover a back or shoulder rub. Almost everybody associates foreplay with sexual contact, but affectionate touch is a great way to prove and rekindle intimacy in a relationship even if you are not much of a touchy-feely individual.

13. Turn off the Electronics

Intense and meaningful emotional intimacy between the couples depends on the quality of their interaction. Texting and emailing are essential ways for you to get useful things done and to stay in touch when you are away from each other and too busy to have an intense communication.

Try turning off the television, computer, video game console, cell phones, and tablet when you are with your partner and spend some time communicating, sharing, and looking at each other in the eye. One tool that many successful people in a relationship use is they put their cell phones on silent mode and drop them in a little basket or box by the door as they come home. All such people believe in spending quality time with each other when they are together.

14. Prioritize Sex above everything

Set the desire for intimate relations before TV or work reduces your passion. A delicious meal, along with your favorite song and wine, can set the stage for perfect sex.

The good thing is that allowing your lover to take charge of you can reignite the spark you once relished. Couples who are familiar with each other intimately [and] are well versed about their likes, dislikes, personality twists, hopes, and dreams are the ones who are enjoying a healthy relationship

Even if you are not an expressive person, by increasing physical fondness and emotional attunement, you can help yourself to sustain a deep, meaningful relationship.

15. Maintain a Balance Between you and your partner.

The strongest & healthy relationships have two mutually dependent partners. Each one has different hobbies, a professional, and social life, and they come together to devote to the Intimate relationship. Too much closeness can be a bad thing if it deprives the connection between the energy and experiences that dependence brings. So, make sure to involve in some good self-care as a father and a husband, and allow your partner to do the same. And then come close to each other as a trusting and secure couple.

Chapter 04: Re-sparkling the Flame of Ownership

Many people mistakenly feel that in a relationship, they are permitted to oversee and control everything about their partner's existence. But that is not the case. When we try to force our will on our partner, the ones we love will become defensive or might consider it as an insult. No one wants to follow the orders, either direct or indirect. Before forcing your loved ones, just try to imagine yourself in their position and think about how you would have behaved in a similar situation.

To avoid such backlash that is associated with this act of imposing, you need to look at the way you are asking. Be very careful in picking the right words. It's quite common that the way you perceive it is different from what your partner has perceived.

Perhaps, it appears like a long process, particularly if you intend to make your partner bring home some milk. But, if you love your partner, this information is for you. You can easily eradicate a significant percentage of your arguments, and sad feelings, by keeping your mouth shut.

The relationship is about the partnership. There is a reason why it is called a partnership. It involves both individuals to have equal controls. No one in a relationship has a right to make the other person submissive. Also, there is psychological reasoning for this. If a couple doesn't treat each other as equals, the love between them won't flow equally, and if that is not happening, you are gradually going to end up in a bad relationship.

By simply converting demands into requests is the best way to initiate. It allows your partner to exercise the right of their free will. The chances of satisfying your needs increase when your loved one feels like they have a choice in this matter.

Acting out by shouting, withholding affection, or just being disgusting is a losing game. It will never help you get what you need. It will only serve to push your lover away. If you think this behavior is acceptable, I appeal to you to ask your partner what he /she is experiencing. Yes, it's a risky situation, but if you do it now, you'll probably save yourself a lot of misery in the future.

What is Ownership in a Relationship?

It is imperative to differentiate between accepting and deflecting responsibility for both the individuals in a relationship. Be careful of defensive reactions, which also include "stop being so sensitive" or "I didn't know that you cared about that," or "you should've done something." It's not only essential for you to take responsibility. Also, your lover must learn and do as well to have a strong relationship.

For you, taking ownership or responsibility looks like practicing self-awareness. Another way is being able to make an apology and accept that what you do affects your lover. For your lover, taking responsibility or ownership looks like having open communication with you about the feelings they have and being willing to confess they can grow from the weak parts of the relationship. Your lover learns to take ownership when they own their behaviors and make themselves accountable for their actions.

Why is it important?

Taking ownership and responsibility for your activities is an essential part of healthy relationships. Doing so is an empowering gesture that you have authority over the role you play in a relationship. Taking responsibility develops trust and dependability. When you start taking responsibility for your actions, you demonstrate to your lover your readiness, to be honest, and vulnerable, which in turn inspires your partner to be open and genuine with you.

It avoids Unhealthy Conflicts

Indicators of unhealthy conflict often emphasize mainly on the needs or expectations of one party. Either with the help of mutual agreement or through compulsion, one person becomes the central focus of the relationship. Meeting that particular set of needs and expectations builds a conspicuous deficit in the notion of mutual fulfillment and creates an emotional storage bin for bitterness and discontent. An unhealthy conflict is also found where there is disrespect for the rights of the other person. Because of the distorted, one-sided focus, a person inappropriately loses rights and undertakes the responsibilities of the other. The confusion that one individual's needs are more important than the other's tips to the mistaken conclusion that this preferred individual's rights proportionately outweigh the other's. when you start taking responsibility or ownership of your actions, you can easily avoid the unhealthy conflicts in a relationship

How lack of ownership spoils a healthy relationship?

At times all relationships will experience characteristics mentioned below. Although unhealthy relationships or relationships with a lack of ownership will display these characteristics more commonly and makes you feel stressed and pressurized and makes it difficult for you to avoid. Such a tense relationship is unhealthy for both the individuals in a relationship and may lead to complications in other aspects of your life.

In a relationship without ownership you:

- *Put one individual before the other one by abandoning yourself or your lover*

- *Feel burdened to change who you are for the other individual*

- *Feel concerned over a disagreement with your partner*

- *Feel burdened to quit activities that you generally enjoy*

- *force the other individual into agreeing with you or indulging into something that suits you*

- *observe one of you has to give justifications like where you go, who you see*

- *Observer one person feels thankful to have sex or has been forced*

- *Don't have privacy, and might be required to share everything with your partner*

- *You or your lover refuse to use safer sex approaches*

- *observe arguments are not fairly settled*

- *observe screaming or physical violence at times during an argument*

- *Try to take charge or manipulate your partner*

- *Observe your lover attempts to take control of how you dress and criticizes your actions*

- *Do not spare time to spend with your lover*

- *Don't have any common friends, or don't have respect for each other's' family and friends*

- *Observe an unbalanced control of resources like food, home, money, car, etc.)*

- *Don't experience anything like fairness and equality.*

Ways to Practice Ownership in Real Life

Every couple in a relationship fights. That's a fact! Some individuals argue all the time, some have big problems infrequently, and some will say, "We don't fight," which is hard to find. But the differentiating factor between working it out together versus calling it quitting comes down to one word: Ownership.

The standard solution for relationship problems seems to be good communication; I have also mentioned the importance of communication in the previous chapters. We emphasize sorting things out. But often, no matter how much we communicate, our problems don't seem to get solved.

To hold oneself responsible means to own one's feelings and taking ownership of one's contribution to the relationship — good and bad. If both people are responsible, one will work at improving their conduct, and the other would work at handling their feelings better. Moreover, it means having the guts to attempt to fix what you messed up, either by seeking for help or applying the correction to change the behavior.

Taking responsibility or ownership is not just a one-sided exercise. The subsequent ways to use the empowering action of taking ownership is important for both you and your lover to use and exercise in your relationship.

1. Be Honest to yourself

"You have to love yourself first before you love others" is a multipurpose phrase that has numerous meanings when applied to relationships. It can interpret to "You have to be honest with yourself before you can be honest with others." Being honest with yourself initiates with a healthy sense of self-awareness. And being self-aware means to acknowledge that what you say and do influences your partner.

2. Don't react to situations, but act

When people are held responsible for their actions, they generally become defensive. Being defensive is a reaction. When you act in a situation, you can reply with clarity and awareness. You can rehearse acting on situations rather than reacting by taking long breaths or counting from 1 to 10. It also helps to take a second and look at the situation from your partner's viewpoint. It can be tough to think from the other perspective, specifically in the heat of the moment. By being honest to yourself and your lover, you can efficiently respond by taking ownership.

3. Be forgiving towards your Partner and Yourself

Everyone commits mistakes and having a forgiving attitude toward your partner or yourself is imperative for moving past challenging situations and making your relationship healthier. When you start taking ownership of your mistakes and consider it as an opportunity to learn, your relationship can become a place that nurtures and celebrates growth. Forgiveness establishes trust and accountability in a relationship; it breaks down resentment and stops the never amusing "blame game."

Taking ownership for your actions in your relationship demands honesty and open communication and also the willingness to address unhealthy justifications with your partner. They're not always relaxed discussions to have, but you'll find that doing so creates trust within your relationship over time and is an empowering way to acquire and grow.

Benefits of Ownership in a Relationship

When you start taking responsibility for your actions, you will begin to experience a range of benefits. The subsequent are some of the benefits you will experience when you start being responsible in a relationship

*1) **Improved Confidence***

Confidence is a relationship, allows you to make things better. Simply put, if a mistake had enough effect of producing a wrong outcome, then doing the right thing will also have enough effect to produce the right outcome

When you start seeing things from a different perspective, you initiate to see how powerful & influential a relationship can be. You start realizing that you can accomplish whatever you want, as long as you are doing the right thing

2) Problem-Solving

If you are not responsible in a relationship, you find it much more difficult to solve any problems in it. The reason for this is quite simple, there are several possible causes of any problem, and by avoiding being accountable, you are refusing to consider one of the possible causes of the problem you experience, and that is your behavior or failure to take action.

3) Healthier Relationship

Have you ever observed how people give anyone an easy time when that person accepts that he/she made a mistake? We all make mistakes. Nobody is perfect, and we all know that. Thus, when someone owns their mistake, we begin to see our reflection in them. When we make mistakes, too, we are more likely to respond with compassion and empathy.

The key point is that it is tougher to create a bond with someone who is not willing to accept his/her mistake. Ownership in a relationship is a great way to strengthen your bond with the people you love.

4) Inspiration

You owe it to your partner to act responsibly. By doing this, you are becoming a role model for them. You are showcasing such strong values which you would want them to develop.

If you want your partner to behave in a certain way, you need to start from yourself. Doing so is the best demonstration of what you are expecting from your partner. Eventually, you will observe fewer conflicts between you and your partner.

Being responsible in a relationship is one way of setting higher standards. When your partner sees that you make yourself responsible for your action, they will have lesser resistance when you make them responsible for their actions too.

5) Improved Decisions

Decision making is also linked with ownership. It's quite simpler to put off making a certain decision because you are worried about the consequences. Your partner is also the one affected by the decision and putting it off; you are not assisting them.

Whereas if you take responsibility in a relationship, you can easily make improved decisions on behalf of your partner as well. It's quite probable you come across different obstacles after making a decision, but your partner will be there to support you in this matter.

Almost everyone takes responsibility for all the good things in a relationship, right? It's quite easy to do that. If you do something good and receive thanks in return, you would feel happy, but the real lovers are the ones who accept their imperfections, express their sorrows, and, most importantly, learn from their faults.

Arguments in an intimate relationship are expected, perhaps unavoidable. From time to time, as two people in a relationship attempt to negotiate the trials and concerns life presents them, they naturally develop contradictory perceptions and differing notions of how best to meet their mutual requirements. What is certainly avoidable is the expression of contradictory views and needs in a manner that is harmful to either party and destructive to the relationship. People who truly care about each other, who grasp each other's best interest at heart, and who value the care and fulfillment of an important intimate relationship, approach argument as a problem to be solved, not a threat to be overlooked or overcome. They find ways to solve the differences while respecting each other and trusting in the power of the relationship as support through the toughest times. Taking ownership for such people often becomes a growth point that serves to strengthen the relationship and makes it ready for future challenges

Chapter 05: Attitudes of Gratitude & Appreciation in a Relationship

Gratitude is essential in any relationship, but specifically between couples. One of the most common issues that couples face is a lack of gratitude and appreciation for their loved ones. When you first meet your loved one, you can't imagine how lucky you are, how sexy your partner is, how funny he/she going to be, how smart they are in general, etc. As time passes by, we become much more comfortable and relaxed in a relationship; we forget to share the gratitude and appreciation with them. Let's talk about how to bring gratitude and appreciation back in a relationship.

Many couples who look for therapy have started to take their partners for granted and do not express appreciation and gratitude towards them for the day to day things that they do to make the relationship healthy and successful. Many of them are just living a normal life, not acknowledging that their lover is making coffee for them every morning, picking the children up from school, taking the dog for long walks. However, these are very little things but can go a long way towards the success of the relationship and the cohesive, smooth running of a partnership or family.

It's not a secret that a relationship requires hard work, and if it is going to work, it demands effort from both the individuals. Although things aren't always the same as peaches and cream, specifically when the honeymoon period ends, if you're in or have ever been indulged in such a relationship, you will identify that at times you can take your lover for granted and vice versa. With time, you might not put in as much energy as you did at the start when the love was fresh and new. Dinner Dates become a thing of the past, and you stop surprising dinners and doing nice things for each other like. This pattern generally leads to a lack of appreciation, and you or both the individuals end up taking each other for granted, believing that just because you have a love for each other, you will always be together.

People in a relationship tend to believe that showing gratitude and appreciation is difficult. They don't know the ways to show it. On the contrary, showing your partner gratitude and appreciation is quite easy to do! Practice makes a man perfect. One of the reasons why your relationship is not smooth is because you are out of practice. Perhaps, you don't know where to start. Here a few ideas that will help you to rekindle the gratitude and appreciation in a relationship.

1. ***Thank your partner for the little things!***

Being thankful in a relationship is indeed imperative. It is one of the most significant habits you can build in a relationship. Gratitude is the main ingredient in any relationship, but it takes pure intentions and time to put it into practice.

Thank your partner over little things, even if it's something you have already expected. Pay attention to small details in which they contribute. Like making dinner or coffee in the morning? Tell them how much you value and appreciate that!

When your lover does certain things for you, it is essential that you acknowledge them. You must cognitively know what your lover is adding to your life, be it something significant or trivial. If you fail to appreciate it, it means you take your partner for granted, and sooner or later, they will identify this too and stop doing what they are doing for. Small gestures like preparing your favorite meal for dinner, or doing your share of the errands or perhaps even something big as planning your birthday; you need to be able to identify these as loving gestures from your lover. However, they may not be looking for praises by doing all of this; if you simply recognize them for their hard work, they will be happy. It will augment love and feeling of gratitude in between the partner.

It's never too late to be thankful! Just remember what your lover has done for you in the past six months – year. Is there anything that they've done that you forgot to show gratitude for? Better late than never!

Being grateful is a way of life, and it carries immense power to endure and boost a relationship when authentic. Gratitude enlightens the good gifts we've been given–both by our partner and by God.

2.   *Express your love for them*

If you do identify your lover's effort, it is equally essential for you to express your gratitude towards them. You must find expressive ways to communicate appreciation that ensure that your lover hears it. For this, the word 'thank you' can be of excessive help. Saying such simple words or writing down on a note is a perfect way to let your lover know that you appreciate them for the efforts they do for you. Likewise, compliments can go a long way and are cool and take no time at all. Saying anything as simple as, 'Dinner was good or 'Thanks for running my errand can be tremendously powerful, positive and kind and can help you improve your relationship and push away all kinds of relationship issues.

3.   *It's time to payback*

Despite feeling and expressing appreciation, gratitude cannot be entirely experienced until reciprocated. You should be returning your lover's favor and making them feel as special as you felt. When both partners start to appreciate each other for all that they do, they generally start a cycle of continuous appreciation and gratitude towards each other. Every one of them will try harder to assist each other due to the positive momentum created for each one to feel loved while also challenged to show appreciation and gratitude towards each other.

4.   *Find reasons to love them*

Gratitude and appreciation help us remember the reasons we first fell in love with our partner. Stating words of gratitude for precious times together and much-loved qualities in one another spark memories of specifically rich seasons that can sustain commitment during harder times. You need to recognize that they love you for who you are. They are the ones who accepted you whole-heartedly. It's just a reason to love your partner. I am sure; when you start finding out, you will discover too many of them.

5.   *Gratitude augments love, fun, and forgiveness.*

Many studies confirm that people who consistently give thanks and appreciate their partners are more likely to experience positive interactions and satisfying emotions. The same goes for a successful marriage. When two individuals are committed to seeing and appreciating life's gifts together, their perceptions change and widens. The anxiety in a relationship tends to lessen, and the sense of enjoyment escalates.

6. *Gratitude develops spiritual intimacy.*

An individual bent toward gratitude receives more graciously, and an individual who feels appreciated gives more confidently. The support of giving and receiving in a healthy marriage reflects the way God's generosity towards his people. When people in a relationship reflects the nature of God by their actions–and they recognize that–a beautiful intimacy occurs. It can be deepened further by giving thanks to Almighty together.

Service is the basic expression of one's spirituality. If attitudes and behaviors of an individual don't change as spirituality matures, the spirituality has likely been built of more artificial substance.

Gratitude and appreciation are natural offshoots of establishing spirituality. Both of them are dependent on each other; one follows and leads to the other. Start working on one, and the other will eventually shadow on its heels — so long as it is not an artificial pretense in disguise.

7. *Gratitude improves Sex-Life*

Truly shared thankfulness strengthens a couple's emotional and spiritual bonds, which undoubtedly fosters a more intense physical relation. When we appreciate one another genuinely, the risk in vulnerability lessens. Affirmation creates a safer environment and a more tender relationship.

8. Gratitude develops a shared cycle of Appreciation.

It's simply a human nature that when an individual feels appreciated, he/she more likely to show appreciation for others. Practicing gratitude in the relationship can have a snowball effect because, as one partner shows thanks and affirmation, the same more logically flows from the other. Occasionally small thanks can lead to a whole and underlying principles of gratitude.

9. Gratitude softens criticism.

Harsh words are painful like a bee-sting, and can easily have the supremacy to tear down confidence in a relationship. When words of appreciation and gratitude become more consistent and integral to a relationship, they slowly build a foundation of trust that cushions the disappointment from harsh words.

Here are some ways or suggestions for practical ways to practice appreciation & gratitude in a relationship:

Make a collective gratitude journal —Together, Note down three things you're each grateful for at the end of every day. Even if it's a tiny thing. Just practice to jot down points that you love about a partner. It is proven by the research that this practice has a substantial impact on happiness among couples.

Pray together —Make a daily routine in which you both come before God, even for a few minutes, and thank Him for one another. Show gratitude towards God that He has given you such a lovely and blessed life. As per the old saying, a family that prays together stays together. It may not always be true; there has some sort of significant correlation. There is an intimacy in prayer when it's spoken soulfully. When you pour out your hearts to God for your family, asking for safety, blessings, comfort, forgiveness, and love, a sacred bond can start to form.

Express through body language —Words are weighty, but appreciation demonstrated in an unspoken manner is influential. Make eye contact every time you say, "thank you." Touch one another affectionately. Complementing a word of thanks with a warm hug or hand-squeeze makes it much more significant.

Reflect the Memories—Appreciate reflecting on memories and times that you've shared. Be actively thankful for the journey you've walked together, stating appreciation for one another and shared experiences.

Praise them in the Public—Another most important thing that many couples think of as less important is praising them in public. Everybody has a different way of praising their partner in public. It could be anything from posting a picture on Facebook or Instagram to praising in general. It will make your partner feel special, and he/she will be genuinely happy. Furthermore, it will also make you remember how lucky you are to be with them.

Exchange the Duties for a Week—The best way to demonstrate your appreciation & gratitude is to show it by your actions. One of the ways you can do that is by exchanging the duties for a week.

Offer to clean the dishes for the week if it was their responsibility, clean up the messy kitchen that day, or pick up the children for the next month so they can see an emphasis on studying for their upcoming exam. Whatever you think they are in charge of, offer to do it for them for some time as a token of appreciation to give them some relief.

Whatever those things are, what you can do for them will be irreplaceable to your relationship, but even small gestures like coming home a little early to make dinner, clean up, or plan a romantic movie night can mean the world to them.

Support them whenever they need it—However, It's challenging to fully understand and know how a person feels, even if they are your long-term partner.

But, if you make an effort, you can tell when anything is bothering them when they feel special, or simply worrying out about a special event or upcoming deadline. And even if you are unable to identify, asking them occasionally when you think they may need help can go a long way.

The point I am trying to deliver is being in a healthy relationship is not just about enjoying each other's company, but it's about supporting your partner, especially when they're having a bad time. That shows your real appreciation and gratitude.

Gifts like chocolate and flowers (for men!)

Certainly, flowers and chocolate can be a bit cliché, but it doesn't mean they are not appreciated well. Women truly like flowers, even if it's just a small expression of thoughtfulness. To make this a little more exceptional, give her flowers daily even when there is not any specific occasion other than expressing your love. An outward demonstration of gratitude with a flower arrangement is excellent when it's unplanned.

Also, if your lady doesn't like flowers, buy her something that almost every other woman in the world adores...chocolates. Buy them chocolate in a heart-shaped box for a special effect. A chocolate bar is not a good option in this case...or perhaps it is.

Focus on minute details

Try to pick up on indirect hints that specify wishful action on your part. Perhaps, it's a nicely spoken word about having the dishes put away, the garage cleaning, the laundry folding, or the car washing. Maybe it's a date night for both of them out of town, or perhaps something that would add to their closet. Whatever it is, pick up the hint and take some action. This is incredibly the most powerful form of gratitude. Focus on details

Disrupt the conventional routine

If you are a woman, does your partner generally take the garbage out? If you are a man, does your woman usually go grocery shopping? These are some clearly defined roles where a bit of switcheroo can allow the gratitude flowing to (and from) your lover... not to mention how special you will feel afterward.

Sure, it might appear like tedious chores to take on, but imagine the surprised look and genuine appreciation on your lover's face when they identify you've done something you hate!

Show gratitude on your success

If you're a lady who received an appraisal, mention how you couldn't have done it without the support of your man. If you are a man who received an appraisal, mention how you couldn't have done it without the help of your lady.

The reality is it doesn't matter what the success is; it is a shared achievement if you're in a committed relationship. You support each other, you have different responsibilities, and each of your hard work and energy makes it possible for the partner you love to make strides in their life.

Be Consistent

Many of us are gifted in showing gratitude from time to time. The actual value lies in being able to demonstrate your gratefulness consistently. Understand this: he or she loves you with all your weaknesses and strengths. The readiness to demonstrate your appreciation for them is well worth the struggle. In fact, you will likely see some form of gratitude and appreciation coming right back at you.

Be more creative in expressing Gratitude—Perhaps

you do tell them you love, appreciate, and also are grateful for your partner. Perhaps, you are saying or doing it the same way so regularly that it's just lost its actual meaning.

If that is the case with you, simply exchanging things up can have the planned effect without any extra effort. We are often deafened by the repetitive actions of our partner after a while, even if the intentions of our partner is pure.

By being creative or switching things up, you can refresh and express your message in a rejuvenating way that allows you to reconnect with your lover.

Conclusion

A romantic and healthy relationship is a two-way interaction, and as such, they are ever-changing and intensely complicated. The recipe for a successful and healthy relationship isn't fully clear, but this book has certainly provided substantial information to show the importance of work and effort. Successful relationships don't just happen overnights: They emerge when two individuals invest in their relationship and have physical and emotional support (e.g., manageable life stress) to do so well. It is worth noting that research on relationship satisfaction and stability focuses on predictors, that plays a vital role in spoiling a beautiful relationship.

Final Words

Thank you again for purchasing this book!

We hope this book can help you.

The next step is for you to **join our email newsletter** to receive updates on any upcoming new book releases or promotions. You can sign-up for free, and as a bonus, you will also receive our "*7 Fitness Mistakes You Don't Know You're Making*" book! This bonus book breaks down many of the most common fitness mistakes and will demystify many of the complexities and science of getting into shape. Having all this fitness knowledge and science organized into an actionable step-by-step book will help you get started in the right direction in your fitness journey! To join our free email newsletter and grab your free book, please visit the link and signup: **www.effingopublishing.com/gift**

Finally, if you enjoyed this book, then we would like to ask you for a favor, would you be kind enough to leave a review for this book? It would be much appreciated! Thank you, and good luck on your journey!

About the Co-Authors

Our name is Alex & George Kaplo; we're both certified personal trainers from Montreal, Canada. We will start by saying we are not the biggest guys you will ever meet, and this has never really been our goal. We started working out to overcome our biggest insecurity when we were younger, which was our self-confidence. You may be going through some challenges right now, or you may simply want to get fit, and we can certainly relate.

We always kind were interested in the health & fitness world and wanted to gain some muscle due to the numerous bullying in our teenage years. We figured we could do something about how our body looks like. This was the beginning of our transformation journey. We had no idea where to start, but we both just got started. We felt worried and afraid at times that other people would make fun of us for doing the exercises the wrong way. We always wished we had a friend to guide us and who could just show us the ropes.

After a lot of work, studying, and countless trials and errors. Some people began to notice how we were both getting more fit and how we were starting to form a keen interest in the topic. This led many friends and new faces to come to us and ask us for fitness advice. At first, it seemed odd when people asked us to help them get in shape. But what kept us going is when they started to see changes in their own body and told us it's the first time that they saw real results! From there, more people kept coming to us, and it made both of us realize after so much reading and studying in this field that it did help us, but it also allowed us to help others. To date, we have coached and trained numerous clients who have achieved some pretty amazing results.

Today, both of us own & operate this publishing business, where we bring passionate and expert authors to write about health and fitness topics. We also run an online fitness business, and we would love to connect with you by inviting you to visit the website on the following page and signing up for our e-mail newsletter (you will even get a free book).

Last but not least, if you are in the position we were once in and you want some guidance, don't hesitate and ask... I will be there to help you out!

Your coaches,

Alex & George Kaplo

Download another book for Free

We want to thank you for purchasing this book and offer you another book (just as long and valuable as this book), "Health & Fitness Mistakes You Don't Know You're Making," completely free.

Visit the link below to signup and receive it:

www.effingopublishing.com/gift

In this book, we will break down the most common health & fitness mistakes, you are probably committing right now, and will reveal how you can quickly get in the best shape of your life!

In addition to this valuable gift, you will also have an opportunity to get our new books for free, enter giveaways, and receive other useful emails from us. Again, visit the link to sign up:

www.effingopublishing.com/gift

Copyright 2019 by Effingo Publishing - All Rights Reserved.

This document by Effingo Publishing, owned by the A&G Direct Inc company, is geared towards providing exact and reliable information in regards to the topic and issue covered. The publication is sold with the idea that the publisher is not required to render accounting, officially permitted or otherwise qualified services. If advice is necessary, legal or professional, a practiced individual in the profession should be ordered.

From a Declaration of Principles which was accepted and approved equally by a Committee of the American Bar Association and a Committee of Publishers and Associations.

In no way is it legal to reproduce, duplicate, or transmit any part of this document in either electronic means or printed format. Recording of this publication is strictly prohibited, and any storage of this document is not allowed unless with written permission from the publisher. All rights reserved.

The information provided herein is stated to be truthful and consistent, in that any liability, in terms of inattention or otherwise, by any usage or abuse of any policies, processes, or directions contained within is the sole and utter responsibility of the recipient reader. Under no circumstances will any legal responsibility or blame be held against the publisher for any reparation, damages, or monetary loss due to the information herein, either directly or indirectly.

The information herein is offered for informational purposes solely and is universal as so. The presentation of the information is without a contract or any type of guarantee assurance.

The trademarks that are used are without any consent, and the publication of the trademark is without permission or backing by the trademark owner. All trademarks and brands within this book are for clarifying purposes only and are owned by the owners themselves, not affiliated with this document.

For more great books, visit:

EffingoPublishing.com

www.ingramcontent.com/pod-product-compliance
Lightning Source LLC
Chambersburg PA
CBHW062141100526
44589CB00014B/1649